GHOST STORIES

Petrifying True Ghost Stories Of The Undead And Their Supernatural Tales

Max Mason Hunter

LIKE BOOKS?

Would you like them delivered to you every week?

Do you like non-fiction books on a huge range of different topics?

We send out e-books every week so we can share our books with the world!

We have books every week on AMAZON that we send to our email list.

So if you want in, then visit the link at the end of this book to sign up and sit back and wait for new books to be sent straight to your inbox!

TABLE OF CONTENTS

Introduction

Chapter 10

Chapter 11

Chapter 12

Conclusion

INTRODUCTION

The world is an infinite place. We don't entirely understand it – we believe in what we see and what we hear and try to make sense of that alone. Things that are easy to quantify, easy to explain with science – some of them are frightening in their intensity, such as a natural disaster, but these things don't keep us up at night from fear. And then, there are those things that we cannot understand.

The complexity of the human mind is such that what it cannot perceive or measure, it fears. And such things do exist – we can hear them, feel them, sense them. But we cannot quantify them, because their behavior does not remain consistent and there seems to be no rational explanation to them.

In this book, we will take a look at the different places and spots on our planet where these inexplicable things exist. Everyone who has been to these places has come back changed; some have even gone just to see for themselves what it's like; their accounts are disturbing.

Some walked away with just chills down their spine and others have had no choice but to accept the diametric shift in the way they now view the world.

This is because what you see and hear in front of you is not all that there is. The world is infinite and the human perception of it is miniscule at best – there are things that we don't understand, elements beyond our comprehension that we cannot truly perceive. Some of these unexplained beings are peaceful, and others are not. Some have reasons to exist – such as unfinished business – and others remain a mystery.

The fact that so many places are rife with such paranormal occurrences is proof that we can't really jump to conclusions and say that the other realm doesn't exist. There are many experts in the field who have devoted their lives to developing that extra sense so that they can commune with these lost spirits; men and women have been to these places and have returned convinced that the spirits want to communicate.

Whether you believe it or not, whether you accept it or not, there are some things in the world that cannot be attributed to anything other than paranormal activity. Some spirits have been through tragedy so heartbreaking, they are trapped within that singular instance that stole their lives away – they relive that moment over and over and over.

Yet others are on the other side of the coin; instead of tragedy, they are trapped by love, unable to leave behind the people who are such an integral part of them.

No matter what the reason for their passing, they haven't really left – they are still here, still waiting for the release of eternal sleep, which is beyond their grasp.

In this book, we will explore the accounts of people who have done research into the history of these haunted places, who have seen for themselves the paranormal, which refuses to be hidden away. Be warned – the stories are not for the faint of heart. Whether you truly feel their presence or it's just the thought that haunts you, remember… we are not alone…

CHAPTER 1

A VILLAGE FELLED – THE ORADOUR-SUR-GLANE MASSACRE

The Second World War was filled with a history so bloody; it's a wonder that we don't have many hauntings related to it. The Nazis murdered millions of innocent people – even if they are not the sites of paranormal activity, these places where the concentration camps existed, still reek of sadness and tragedy.

In France, there exists a small village where an entire community was slaughtered like sheep. It is one of the few sites of Nazi Massacres that has not been restored to its former glory – it serves as a reminder that humans can be the most depraved of creatures and that we can descend into a condition that is worse than animals, who at least attack only when provoked.

On the 10th of June in the year 1944, Oradour-sur-Glane was attacked – an entire village was needlessly slaughtered and only a handful of survivors escaped. Despite the fact that they were little more than children and shouldn't really be able to remember much of their past, these survivors were traumatized for life and even now, shudder at the nightmares that plague them.

What is horrific is the senseless murder of innocents – it wasn't even the Oradour-sur-Glane village that the Germans were after. The French Resistance had made another village, Oradour-sur-Vayres, their headquarters to operate out of.

The Germans, believing that Oradour-sur-Glane was the village,

1

attacked these people instead, indiscriminately shooting and even burning the citizens alive.

Despite the horror of war, one could possibly understand taking a rebel village and fighting soldiers, who would have at least died defending what they believed. But these people were innocent bystanders who were murdered because some official in the German army made the mistake of reading the wrong name. It is a disturbing thought indeed.

Almost 650 people were killed, out of which more than 200 were young children. The entire village was torched. Today; the ruins still stand as a reminder of the depravity that humankind can descend into. What's sad is that the villagers had remained neutral in the war; they had no idea that the neighboring village was a hub of Resistance activity or that the Nazis were anywhere close by.

One can, perhaps, blame the German commander, Adolf Diekmann, for the needless deaths that day – he'd been constantly defeated by the French Rebel troops that were housed in the next village and he wanted to get rid of them as soon as possible. He didn't bother to make sure that he was attacking the right village and in the process, massacred hundreds of peaceful, innocent people.

He called together his entire regiment on the 10th of June early in the morning and they entered the village. They called for all the people to come to the fairgrounds, which was called the Camp de Foire.

Claiming that people should come to complete this routine checkup of identity papers, they managed to get all the residents together and then separated them into two groups – the men on one side and the women and the kids on the other.

The men were split into smaller factions and taken to barns and warehouses, hangars and garages. In the meantime, the second group was taken to the village church; on the way, the Nazis even made the children sing happily, such was their sadism. As soon as the women and children entered the church, they heard the sound of several machine guns being fired – the men in the barns were simultaneously shot in the legs and left immobile.

Within moments, those in the church could smell and see the smoke; the Nazis set fire to the barns were these poor men were trapped, unable to escape with their shattered legs. Stuck in the fires, they soon choked to death.

Five of the men managed to escape the horror – soon after their fellow men died, the Nazis came to check on them. These five men hid within the dead and then crawled to the bushes, where they hid out until the next day.

In the meanwhile, the women and children were trying to escape as well. They were struggling against the soldiers who kept them captive inside the church – a gas bomb was placed to make sure they wouldn't escape. However, the bomb went wonky and didn't go off; a number of the group managed to get out, but they were not spared.

Instead, the soldiers shot them with the same machine guns that had destroyed the men. Those still inside the church were burnt alive as another grenade was thrown in and the place was set fire to.

Within the space of a few hours, an entire community was gone – the Nazis came back to check for survivors, looted their homes as the spoils of war and then, to be sure that there wouldn't be survivors, they burnt down every building so that the village would be utterly razed. Then, they went their merry way. Only 20 people or so managed to escape this mass butchering.

Man, woman, child, and adult – it made no difference to them whom they were killing. They simply torched the entire place, leaving behind no survivors and then went on ahead with their war effort, not even caring to check if they'd gotten the right target.

Today, the locals call the village 'The Village of the Martyred', and for good reason. None of them will dare to go there at night – when they look out of their windows; they can see heavy shadowy figures that walk around the ruined village. More than one local has seen these silhouettes wandering around the ghost town.

A few years later, in 1958, a new Oradour-sur-Glane was constructed, just on the edge of the ghost town. The people of this village have had their encounters with the paranormal – they can often smell the stench of wood burning when they walk across the village at night.

And it isn't just burning wood — the stench of burning flesh also clogs the air, proving that the spirits of the innocents murdered are still trapped here.

A tradition has since developed among the locals — the new villagers leave presents for their massacred elders on the borders of the ruined ghost town. This was an attempt on their part to appease these tortured spirits that are trapped within, to show them that they are not forgotten.

These spirits have not been properly put to rest as they should have been — the villagers believe that this is the least they can do for those who ended up being collateral damage in a war they wanted nothing to do with.

CHAPTER 2

OKIKU – THE DEATH OF LOYALTY

Built in the heart of the city of Himeji in Japan, the Himeji Castle is one of the most famous hotspots within the country. It stands on the peak of a tall hill, which means that it can be seen from anywhere within the area. The locals call it the 'White Heron Castle' because it has a pale white exterior that can be seen from miles away.

With over 83 rooms, the Himeji Castle is one of the three biggest castles within the country; it goes without saying that it gets a lot of visitors. But it isn't just its grand interiors and its structure that people want to see – curious minds want to explore the truth behind its ghost stories and find out for themselves if there truly is paranormal activity taking place behind its walls.

Built in the early 14th century, the castle was originally christened the Himeyama Castle. It was the home of Lord Himeji, who wanted a safe place to stay. The dense woods and jungle that surrounded the area was perfect cover, he felt, and thus, had it built as a secure place for himself.

The castle's history is rife with horror and tragedy. A young girl named Okiku was a servant in the castle in early times, and she worked in the dungeons. Now, the dungeons were built in the deepest depths of the mountain that the castle stood on – this meant that she ventured into the heart of the hill almost every day.

Okiku's master was a man named Tessan Aoyama – he was a very well known and successful samurai. He and his wife possessed ten

5

plates made of gold that were extremely valuable.

To keep these Dutch plates safe and secure, they hired Okiku, whose primary purpose was to guard them carefully. Even today, this area of the castle is known to all as 'The Plate Mansion'.

As is the norm with these tales, Aoyama took a liking to the young maid. His wife was fond of Okiku, and trusted her with her most prized possessions – Okiku herself was loyal to her mistress and did not respond to Aoyama's advances.

He pestered her and promised her that he would leave his wife for her if she only chose to accept his proposal – Okiku repeatedly refused, steadfast in her loyalty to her lady and expected that as a samurai who had a code of honor, he would take the rejection gracefully and back off.

But Aoyama was not a man of honor, it would seem. Angry that a servant girl such as herself had refused him, he decided to teach her a lesson. And so, he planned to avenge the insult he had suffered – he took one of the golden plates away and hid them. Okiku, who guarded the plates with her very life, began to look for them franticly, terrified of having lost it.

Tessan went to her then and boasted that he had the plate with him; if she did not consent to be his lover, he would have her outed as a thief. He would put the blame on her and she would be executed for stealing from her own mistress. Who would believe a servant girl over a samurai of such power such as him?

Okiku sobbed and pleaded with him, but he refused to let her go. In despair, unable to do anything, she made the only choice she could – she jumped into the well that was located in the courtyard and killed herself. She certainly didn't want to be forced into being the lover of a man as horrific as Aoyama and she didn't want to betray her mistress. And so, she chose to take her own life in an attempt to escape her fate.

And Tessan reacted as you would expect of a man like him – he kept the plate with himself and publicly blamed Okiku, claiming that she had taken her own life in guilt.

Even today, tourists swear that they can see the shattered Okiku wandering around the castle walls, in search of that peace that eludes her. Locals believe that her spirit has become a Yurumi; a Yurumi is the ghost of a person who passed away under unfortunate circumstances.

A Yurumi has thick black hair and is dressed in white. What distinguishes a Yurumi from other spirits is the way her hands and/or her feet are – they are either missing completely or they are dismembered. All those who felt the presence of Okiku have seen this form, lonely and forlorn and shattered.

Local legend says that this spirit of Okiku is still searching for the lost plate – every night, she would climb out of the well and return to the castle, where she would search franticly for the plate that belonged to her mistress. She would count the plates in the castle and when there were only nine instead of ten, she would return to the well with a loud wail, screaming and sobbing for Tessan to return the tenth.

This continued for years, even when Aoyama was alive – but not once did he attempt to appease her, too proud to admit his crime.

Eventually, being haunted by the woman whose death he'd caused became too much for the samurai; he went insane and took his own life. He also jumped into the well and plunged to his death – Okiku had her revenge by killing him the same manner as he had killed her. But for spirits, there is no end, even in revenge. Okiku's spirit awaits rest, for she still wanders around, searching for the lost plate.

The loud screaming and wailing have startled tourists, as they visit the castle. She is still looking for the item she was charged to guard with her life, the locals say, and she laments her unfair fate daily.

The legend of the young maid is so famous in Japan that it has even been performed as a play. The story, however, has many different versions – but the single strand that connects all of them is the senseless tragedy that took a young woman's life and left her lost in the other realm. Over the years, the sightings have gone down in number, but the well where she drowned – Okiku's Well – still has a sense of pain and sadness about it.

What's interesting is that unlike most haunted areas, this one doesn't seem to bring bad luck. On the contrary, it brings good luck to those who come here – having survived a number of wars and fights, it belongs to the Japanese government today, which has declared it a cultural sight and keeps it protected.

For instance, a bomb during the Second World War landed in the castle. But it's luck was such that the bomb didn't go off and the castle stood strong, undisturbed and proud. People who go there return home to find wonderful surprises waiting for them; the sense of sadness and desolateness about the place reminds them that they should learn to live life and enjoy it while they can because it's so short.

Is it that Okiku is still protecting the castle with her own sense of self? She was an intensely loyal woman; instead of betraying her mistress, she killed herself, choosing duty and self-respect over riches and money. Is it that she wants to extend this sense of duty and loyalty to all those who visit? We can only imagine...

CHAPTER 3

'SAGE'LY MURDERS AT CHILLINGHAM CASTLE

Castles tend to have long and bloody histories that fire up your imagination. Some are haunted, some are not, but they all possess dark stories that you just cannot help but wonder about.

Now, in the northern part of England, on the border between England and Scotland, there is a castle. Its history has been disturbing since the medieval times, simply because this castle was a strategic point in the war that was taking place between the English and the Scots during the 14th century.

The castle boasts a huge dungeon that has been built right below it. The dungeon is infamous – it has earned its reputation as being one of England's most notorious torture chambers. Almost 7500 Scots – men, women and children, indiscriminately – were tortured and murdered within this very chamber. For three long years, they were held there and tortured until they were finally killed.

As I said before, the castle was located in a strategic position, which meant that the English were going to defend it viciously. It became a source of scuffle between the English and the Scots – King Edward's troops made the castle the point of entry into Scotland from England, and in retaliation, the Scots, under the leadership of William Wallace, attacked the castle at frequent intervals.

As you can guess, the torture chamber is definitely the culprit behind the multiple hauntings at this site. The silence is so heavy and chilling that locals swear that they can hear the sound of the last breaths of the victims who were murdered here.

Trapped and left abandoned but for their tormentors, the prisoners used to draw marks on the walls to keep count of how long they had been there – days blended into months and months into years and without these marks, they might have forgotten the outside world altogether.

You can still see these marks there even today.

These victims were tortured senselessly – prisoner of war or not, they were not afforded the mercy of a quick death. The torture devices used were horrific; thumbscrews and chains, racks and iron maidens, mantraps and the like were commonplace and drove the prisoners within an inch of insanity.

They were made to sit on chairs with leather spikes and on beds of nails; they had their eyes gouged out and were tied to a spike barrel that was kicked down a hill until the prisoners' flesh came off.

If that horror isn't enough for you – a starved rat in a cage was tied to the victims' stomachs. The rat would nibble its way through the poor prisoner's stomach, who could only watch in horror as they were being eaten alive. And then, to make sure that the blood and the leftovers didn't ruin the castle, the dungeons were built on a slope with a trench at the end – the remains would literally be just drained and flushed out.

A twenty-foot oubliette existed, into which people were thrown. They were left to starve inside – after going months without food, some resorted to cannibalism and ended up eating the chunks of flesh off of their fellow prisoners.

Others ate their own flesh in an attempt to survive; to this day, one can see the bones of the last victim – a female child – thrown into the oubliette. Visitors have seen the ghost of the child staring back at them from inside; it's terrified more than one local...

And obviously, a place like this is haunted – strange noises, weird flashes of light, an eerie sense of disquiet and danger lingers, frightening tourists and locals alike. When the staff and visitors take pictures within these chambers, the photos have strange lights within them that indicate paranormal activity. The guides who take the tourists on their journey refuse to step into the chambers by themselves – they feel the malevolence of the spirits trapped inside and are terrified of their rage.

For instance, take the man who oversaw the tortures themselves. John Sage was once a distinguished soldier in the war, who could no longer fight because he was injured. Still wanting to serve his country, he requested a second posting from the King, who promptly made him the torturer at Chillingham Castle.

He sounds like a man of patriotism, but in reality, he was a brute – he hated the Scots so much that he ensured that at least 50 of them would be killed in the torture chambers each week. He came up with many of the techniques used to torture them and he did it, not to pull information out of them, but simply because he didn't consider them to be people and hated them utterly.

When the war came to an end, one would think that the prisoners would at least be let go then. But Sage simply dragged them out to the courtyard and then pushed them all into the bonfire.

In this crowd were all the older children and the men and the women – the younger kids had been placed in a room in the castle called the 'Edward's Room'. The room was located on the top floor of the castle and from there, they were forced to listen in anguish as their parents burnt to death. They could hear the screams and smell the burning flesh, as the fire crackled across their families' skin.

Mad was John Sage – he was convinced that these kids would want revenge and then proceeded to chop them all to death using an axe once he'd finished burning their families. Today, this has become the most haunted spot within the castle – chandeliers and furnishings rattle angrily on their own.

People can hear soft, tortured cries and footsteps racing out, trying to escape a madness that has been trapping them for centuries now. And no wonder – can you imagine the horror of watching your family be burnt alive and then being hacked to pieces with a bloody axe?

11

You'd think that Sage's end would put an end to his madness – it didn't. As he was having sex with a woman on the torture rack, he accidentally killed her. Elizabeth Charlton, however, was the daughter of a very powerful man – he was a member of the Border Reevers and he threatened the King that if Sage wasn't punished, he would leave England and join the Scots in battle.

The Reevers were not to be taken lightly; the King agreed instantly and had Sage brought to trial, and then executed.

Sage's death was public – he was hung from a tree on the grounds of the very castle that he murdered so many. People watched with enthusiasm as he breathed his last; even his very presence seemed to breathe violence and rage. Rumor has it that each and every one of his fingers and toes were cut off as torture and then the onlookers took these pieces home as a souvenir of the most evil man they had known.

Obviously, the spirit of Sage haunts the castle to this day. Where the other spirits invoke a sense of tragedy and horror at their needless deaths, Sage definitely inspires terror and fear in his wake, just as he did even in his lifetime.

800 years old and left open to the public, the castle even hosts events and invites guests. But it is a paranormal hotspot, so much so that the staff has a paranormal team living with them to keep these monsters at bay.

They conduct night vigils that the curious tourists often join; few are able to respond at the end of their night stay, so traumatized are they by it all.

CHAPTER 4

REIGNING HELL-FIRE AT THE MONTPELIER HOUSE

The Montpelier House was built in the 18th century. It was constructed to be the hunting lodge of the Speaker of the House of Commons from Ireland, but according to the locals, the house was damned from the moment it was built.

It served as the hunting lodge it was supposed to be only for a short while; soon after, the Irish Hell Fire Club took to using it as their meeting place.

The very name – Irish Hell Fire Club – can give you an idea as to what kind of activities they carried out here. The most depraved of acts, the evilest and cruelest things you and I can think of, were undertaken here, leading the house to become one of the most haunted places within the world. With the Hell Fire Club, it's said that the Devil himself walked the halls of the house.

One night, the members of the club were all gathered together and playing cards. It was stormy outside and the candles kept flickering from the harsh wind – lightning flashed across the sky and lit the room up for moments before plunging it back into darkness. It was at this point that they heard a sudden knock on the door.

You or I would have jumped out of our skins, but these men were made of hard stuff; they thought it was just another one of their club members coming to join their game.

Add to that the fact that the members of this club were wealthy and

13

influential people – they had power within the land, as barons and lords who didn't just get turned away when they knocked on the door; instead, they were welcomed with honor.

What's interesting to note is that there was a spot at the table reserved for this man – but not all the members were aware that he was expected. Still, he joined the ongoing game and together, the men had a very good time. The unknown stranger did not say much, but those who knew him and of his arrival didn't expect him to.

The other members just wanted someone to play the game with them; they were excited about having a new person to show them a new style of playing cards. The game went on – one member dropped his cards to the floor...

Embarrassed that he could be so stupid, he bent down to yank the cards to himself, only to get the shock of his life. As he gathered the cards up, he happened to get a glimpse of the stranger's feet – they were utterly misshapen.

More than that, they didn't look human; they looked like the hooves of a beast. Shaken, the man mumbled to himself and went back to his seat. The guest, however, knew that his cover had been blown – he stood up and vanished, leaving behind a strong, disgusting stench.

The guest was none other than the Devil. And since this instance, the Hell Fire Club has been called 'The Kennel' and 'The Shooting Club'.

To give you a bit more about the history of the house – in the year 1725, the Speaker of the House of Commons, William Connolly, built the house in Dublin County in Ireland. The material to build the house was sourced from stone quarries – as they began construction, people stated that there was this sense of doom and danger about the place. These warnings went unheeded; perhaps, they should have listened.

The workers, as they were digging the land so that they could lay down a stable foundation for the house to rest on, came across something strange. There was an old passageway that they followed all the way to a burial place – a cairn.

This isn't anything new; burial places are often inlaid in residential areas and if left alone, they're hardly going to disturb anyone. But William Connolly made the mistake of disturbing it; he ordered that the house have large stones inlaid into its structure. The workers took a stone that had been used in a sacred resting place and then turned it into the lintel that was then used for the fireplace inside the house.

Locals claim that this is when the house was cursed – and for good reason! But it didn't stop there. The moment construction of the house came to an end; the entire slate roof was blown clear out. And what did the workers use to replace it? That's right, they took the stones from the top of the cairn to finish it. Is it any wonder that the house is haunted then?

Connolly died soon after and then six years passed with the house being abandoned. Finally, it was leased out to the Hell Fire Club, which was started as a normal gentleman's club at the time.

When it began in 1719, it wasn't as bad; while their motto was 'Do what you want', I doubt it was begun as the depraved manic club it ended up being. However, they *did* insist that the people who join their club not worry about doing immoral things or taking part in lewd activity.

Perhaps the seeds of madness were already sown, and then brought to life within the walls of the haunted house. Given the remoteness of the Montpelier Castle, it's hardly surprising that 'doing what they wanted' quickly went from stealing and sex to utter madness – orgies and drunkenness catapulted into occult, devil worship, human and animal sacrifice, torture for pleasure and the like.

Did the spirits of the desecrated cairn exact their revenge on humanity by turning the men on to such heinous acts? Or were the men already depraved and did their victims add to the misery of the house?

The most infamous story related to the Club comes from the accounts of several people. One of the meetings turned horrific; a normal drinking session then turned into a fire that almost destroyed the entire house. It started as a small accident, but like with most tragedies, it bludgeoned into a horrific response that caused the fire. A man named Richard Whaley is often cited to be the cause of the fire.

As a man who was staunchly against religion, this Club member took it to the extreme – he went about setting fire to the Catholic chapels every Sunday. He soon became infamous for it. On the day the accident took place, all the Club members were lying on the floor, drunk and lost. They had just completed a black mass and finished the ceremony with their usual drinks.

A footman was clearing the place up, like always, and as he tried to maneuver around the drunken forms lying haphazardly on the floor, he slipped and ended up spilling some brandy across Whaley's coat.

You can see why the Devil walked the halls of the house from the man's reaction to that – where you or I would have, at worse, yelled at the man and fired him from his job, Whaley fired him literally...

He poured the brandy all over the man and then set fire to him. Yelling in pain and fear, the footman ran down the stairs and died, clinging to the tapestry that was hanging near a door of the hall. The fire caught and began to spread to the entire house, leaving the building beyond repair.

Eventually, the Connolly family sold the house to the White family, who then sold it again to the Massy family, who finally gave it to the State. Today, the house is government property and is maintained by the Forestry Department.

After the fire, the Hell Fire Club stopped using the Montpelier House as their headquarters and shifted to the Killakee Stewards House, where they continued their acts of depravity and sin. The Montpelier House saw so much of it that it became engulfed with negative energy and evil – human depravity leaves a mark and the locals and visitors who have seen the insides of the house have experienced the dark remnants.

Unseen hands tap at the shoulders of those who dare to walk into the house, pulling at necklaces and chains, almost choking the visitors. Strange sounds, like footsteps, are common and just the sight of the ruins themselves is enough to send chills down anyone's spine.

Is it the angry cairn spirits that are longing to return to rest? The burial ground is still present right below the house; is it that they just want to go back home and return to where they were disturbed from?

Or is it the victims, like that innocent footman, who are now exacting vengeance for a death that came upon them too early in the only way they know how? We can only speculate at the horrors.

Trope though it may sound like, a number of people have seen a random black cat wandering around the halls of this house. During one of the sacrifices the Club was making to the Devil, the cat had apparently wandered into the house. It became possessed after that instance and had to be exorcised by a priest – is the spirit of the cat still walking, unable to return from whence it was called?

The Hell Fire Club was pure evil – they enjoyed causing pain and misery to others every time they met at the house. For instance, they liked to torture people for fun. There are rumors that they once put a woman in a barrel, after which they set the barrel ablaze and rolled it down a hill, just because it was so much fun.

What kind of sick mind wants to cause such misery?

Visitors who have had the guts to stay the night at this house have heard that woman screaming for help – when they try to find here, there's nothing but empty silence and an eerie sense of something not right. The presence of the woman is still there; she is trapped as are all the spirits within the house – lost, in fear and waiting for a release that may never come.

The Hellfire Club reined hell on earth and from their depravity stemmed a place so evil; people are terrified to even walk close to it today. Human madness and anger can leave a dark mark and in Montpelier House, this mark is clearly visible.

CHAPTER 5

A MAN SCORNED AT THE WOLFSEGG CASTLE

Picture it – a small, quaint little village in Bavaria that boasts of a wonderful castle that you can visit on your getaway holiday with your entire family. A weekend of fun, relaxation and unwinding. There's only one problem - the castle is haunted. And it isn't a gag joke.

Wolfsegg Castle has attained infamy over the years it has stood, not least because of its tragic history alone. It's a landmark in the area, for all the wrong and mysterious reasons. Like any other castle, it's story is filled with drama and horror, only unlike other castles; the tragedy has stayed behind to the dismay of the local dwellers, tourists and all visitors.

A simple story of a man and woman, Lady Klara Von Helfenstein married a man named Ulrich von Laaber and together, they tended the castle, which was actually meant as a home for travelers.

Ulrich, as you can probably guess, was no ordinary man – he was a knight, which meant that he was often away from home, fulfilling his duties in the army and taking up call as an ambassador. Not wanting to leave his beloved wife all by herself, he asked for a man named Georg Moller to look after her when he was away.

As with all such tragic tales, Klara grew lonely – she called Moller to her bed and made love to him. Moller, who had long since had a rivalry with Ulrich, went eagerly; he was a business owner within the locality and wasn't without power of his own.

When the news of his wife's betrayal reached him, Ulrich found himself too heartbroken to want to return to the castle. Still, he wasn't one to take such humiliation lightly; he wanted to punish the transgressions of the people he'd loved so dearly, who'd dared to betray him in such a derogatory manner. He hired two farmers to kill his wife.

The hired assassins succeeded – Klara was killed.

But Ulrich was unable to defeat his rival, Georg. As a powerful businessman in the locality, he was well protected, and no assassin could actually touch him. What's interesting to note is this – apparently, soon after Klara's death, the man vanished under mysterious circumstances. He walked into the woods and never returned.

Soon after Georg disappeared, Ulrich returned to his castle, bringing his sons along with him. Here's the kicker – the day they arrived, they all went missing. Nobody saw them leave the place, nor were their bodies ever found. They also vanished, just as Georg had.

It goes without saying that a history as bloody as this is bound to have left some remnants behind. While many people want to believe that nothing is within the castle, still others want to explore the truth; having been converted into a museum, the castle is now open to all and is a tourist spot.

But a fun tour it is not. Visitors have seen the apparition of the 'Lady in White', in whose presence all kinds of strange things happen. Inanimate objects began to rattle around and moved on their own, as though a poltergeist was moving them.

Poltergeists and The Lady in White are ancient supernatural creatures that we have encountered repeatedly over the centuries. The woman in white, particularly, is one of the most common apparitions that people have come across. One of the earliest stories we know of the woman in white is the La Llorona, from Mexico, whose story is just as disturbing as Klara.

Translated into English as 'The Sobbing Woman', La Llorona was a woman who loved a man passionately, but was repeatedly rejected by him. Even after bearing him a number of children, he refused to marry her – he killed her and the kids and then ran away.

Rumor is that La Llorona still roams the earth in a tattered white dress that drips in red blood, crying for the children she lost.

If La Llorona was one tragedy, Klara was another. Wolfsegg Castle, however, isn't just the site of the White Woman; it's more disturbing than even that. And this horror lies in the woods behind the castle, where Georg vanished.

When you walk into the woods for about a 100 yards or so, you will come upon a cave; it's been named 'The Hole' by the people who live there. The name itself serves as a warning for all to stay away – the cave itself is steep, plunging into darkness and into what seems like a never-ending hole.

And from this hole come strange sounds. Heavy breathing, disturbing grunts that aren't even human in nature, intense growls and even snarls – all these are regularly heard!

The locals are terrified of 'The Hole' because anyone who goes in to investigate the source of the sound has never returned. For the past 8 centuries, since the death of Klara and the disappearance of Georg, Ulrich and his sons, this has been the reality.

A number of people from the scientific community believed that it was all hogwash and decided to refute the local claims of paranormal activity. An expedition was organized in the 1920s to identify the source of the sounds. They weren't completely successful, but they did come up with a number of theories that could explain the noises.

Geologists and naturalists said that the sounds could come from an animal that had made the hole it's den. This makes sense; the only problem is that no animal could actually climb in or out of the hole, given how steep it is.

In the end, it was concluded that there must be a second entrance to the cave, through which the animal got in and out. And they were right – there *was* a second entrance.

Only, it was even steeper than the first, and it did not allow for any kind of movement at all. This meant that the hole had very little horizontal surface – it goes only downwards, which, for a cave, is not only unnatural, but also disturbing.

The second theory that popped up was that hunters were using the hole as a hiding spot for their goods and scaring people away. Again, an interesting theory, backed up by the animal skeletons – including that of a bear – that were found here.

But the human skeletons are unexplained; did that mean that the hunters – who wanted only animals – killed human beings also? The theory raises more questions than answers, for if there have been more murders here; it's no surprise that there are hauntings.

Even today, the source of the strange growls and snarls remains a mystery. After 1969, when the investigations were at a peak, the searches trailed off; too many people vanished, were injured or hurt in the course of it and the search was abandoned. However, paranormal experts have confirmed the presence of the Lady in White. An unhappy young woman walks the castle in tears, wailing for something she's lost.

Locals will always fear The Hole and advise against going close to it; science hasn't declared it safe even after all investigations and searches. No hunter uses caves to hide his 'stash' anymore and what animal species would use the same cave as home for over *800* years? Paranormal, then, seems to be the only explanation.

Is it Klara, angry to have been murdered, despite her adultery? Is it Georg, perhaps killed or perhaps died of heartbreak after his lover was murdered? Is it Ulrich or maybe even his sons, who could have been killed by an angry spirit and are unable to leave themselves now?

The tragedy of human decisions and the consequences these choices could have – has turned what was supposed to be a place of rest and safety for travelers, into a place of anger, horror and death.

The locals may accompany the tourists into the woods, but they refuse to step close to The Hole, because they know – we are not alone and we can never truly understand the world fully.

CHAPTER 6

NO LONGER RESTING AT THE LOTHIAN CEMETERY

Cemeteries have always been enough to invoke a sense of fear into people – burial grounds, for good reason, are always sites of superstitious beliefs. Paranormal sightings in these places and around them are more often than not exaggerated, simply because something about the dead fires up our imagination. After all, walking into the graveyard at midnight has always been a trope and a dare.

But the Lothian Cemetery in India is a bit different – after sunset, there is true horror that resides in this place and it takes nerves of steel to be able to go anywhere near it. Whether ghosts truly exist or not is still up for debate; most people who claim to have seen them with their own eyes are too traumatized to talk about it.

And the skeptics jump in, claiming that the bizarre things can be explained – and yet others say that ghosts are things that science just hasn't found an explanation for or hasn't advanced enough to understand. Whatever you want to believe, the fact remains that there are unexplained things in this world – the Lothian Cemetery is one of these things.

Close to the Kashmere Gate in New Delhi of India, this cemetery is infamous for its hauntings and poltergeist activities. There is controversy behind the cemetery – it's been charged for land encroachment. Some homeless people have found temporary shelters within the cemetery, poverty having pushed them into living amongst the dead.

But it's the history of the cemetery that we need to take a look at. Built back in the time when India was still a British colony, this is a graveyard that is almost 200 years old. But that's what the records say – conspiracy theorists say that the British stole the cemetery from the Moghuls ruling over the area.

It was believed to have been a Muslim Burial Ground that the royals in Delhi used to bury their dead; once the British entered, they began to use it as their own and soon made it one of the oldest Christian cemeteries in Delhi.

What's tragic about this story is not the way the cemetery changed hands, but the desecration of the dead that was carried out by the British. For they didn't just dig fresh graves for their own, they decided to dig out already existing graves and unearth the corpses of the 'lowly' Indians, whom they did not want their people to lie next to for all eternity.

The vandalized graves were then remade – the dead so unearthed were returned to their families and then asked to be buried elsewhere. Soon, it became such that the cemetery was an English Only Graveyard, to the point where the very name of the cemetery was made English.

The origin of the name is unclear; it's thought to have been named either after the first Englishman buried here or the officer in charge of the whole dirty operation.

One of the most important occurrences at this graveyard was the burial of the soldiers who were killed in the Sepoy Mutiny of India in the year 1857. This was the first major attempt on behalf of the Indians to throw the British out of their country; it was a blood massacre in which hundreds of people were killed. At the end of it, the English soldiers who died were buried in this cemetery.

The Indian sepoys were not buried here. A large cross, with an inscription that read, *"This cross is sacred to the memory of those whose nameless graves lie around"* was installed, along with the words, *"In memoriam MDCCCLVII"*, which is translated as 'In Memory of 1857'.

Are the restless Indian soldiers, who fought for the British and were given no recognition even then, still roaming around?

Are the hauntings the result of the Indians who were massacred for asking for their own freedom? Or are they spirits of the desecrated, who are angry at having their rest so rudely awoken? We can only speculate.

Of the many tales that surround this graveyard, some are infamous. There was Sir Nicholas, who fell in love with an Indian woman. Since she was already married to another man, she refused his advances. Heartbroken, Sir Nicholas then proceeded to kill himself by shooting himself in the head.

Like all Englishmen in Delhi at the time, he too was buried at Lothian Cemetery. Today, locals swear by the existence of his apparition – he walks around forlornly in the night, calling out for his beloved in an eerie voice. Some say that this apparition has a distorted head; others have seen the figure walk around with his head in his own hands!

And if Sir Nicholas wasn't enough, a young boy loiters around in the graveyard after the sun sets. He comes every night after it turns dark and franticly searches for something – when someone asked him what he was looking for, he cried that he couldn't find his parents, who had been buried right there.

And then the boy vanishes – is he a desecrated spirit, trying to find his way home? For there seems to be no evidence of his existence; every attempt to find his real home has failed and he doesn't appear in the daylight.

Interestingly, the locals who live next to the cemetery claim that they have become used to the hauntings. They aren't surprised when a random apparition appears, either in the getup of a British soldier or even as a Moghul warrior, giving credibility to the theory that this was once a Muslim Burial Ground. After all, the British may have desecrated the graves and removed the bodies, but the souls of the people put to rest here haven't moved. They remain at the place they were laid to rest at, but are they at peace even now? We don't know.

Some say that these stories have been made up to make sure that the graveyard is not demolished. Whether that is true or not doesn't change the fact that the cemetery certainly has an interesting – and bloody – history. The fact remains; too many people have seen strange apparitions within the area, and there are too many unexplained instances that can't be ignored.

Rudely awakened from their slumber, it's no wonder that these spirits are trying to escape! The locals will forbid you from entering the graveyard – they know what it's like to make sense of the beyond and are smart enough not to try it. Explorers who wanted the truth went in and came out traumatized, unable to share anything with the world.

Whether we believe in it or not, there is something there. The cemetery is cold – too cold to be normal – and there is an eerie sense of fear and danger that surrounds the whole place. Homeless people who take shelter there have little to say; they are too traumatized, both by their own helplessness as well as the unexplained infinite they encounter each night.

We only know of the stories the locals spread – what is the truth, can we truly know?

CHAPTER 7

THE WRECKED TALE OF THE ALKIMOS

There is something about a shipwreck that strikes the imagination – if it's not the possibility of a hidden treasure; it's definitely the chance of a haunting. And with good reason.

Experience has shown us that shipwrecks tend to be hotspots of paranormal activity; many a time, people have dived down to check for supernatural activities and come up changed, having caught sight of apparitions and eerie spirits down in the wreck. The infamous Titanic is has been explored a number of times for such paranormal activity.

But where The Titanic seems to pull in only tourists, The Alkimos Shipwreck is a true mystery spot; it boasts of one of the most active hauntings on the planet. Submerged in the murky waters off the West Australian Coast, this wreck is scary at best and terrifying at worst.

The Alkimos was wrecked in the year 1963, just to the north of Perth, located in Western Australia. Today, this vessel – once a proud merchant ship – is now known as the cursed and jinxed machine, because bad things happen every time people go to see it.

The wreck itself is a disturbing sight; strange apparitions make themselves known around the area where the vessel sank and tourists have been terrified by weird visions that they don't know what to make of.

The story of the ship begins with the Second World War. At this time, around 2750 Congress Liberty Ships were ordered to be made with America's approval. One of many, The Alkimos was initially christened George M Shiver, and then renamed Viggo Hansteen after the war ended, at which point, it was sold off to the Norwegians.

As Viggo Hansteen, in 1944, she had a close call. As they headed to the Russian port, the crew of Hansteen were attacked by powerful German U Boats – two other merchant ships were bombed as well. Stranded on a reef, Viggo Hansteen had to wait a full six hours before she broke free of the reef without much help.

It was after this that she was sold to the Greeks, who gave her the name The Alkimos. For almost twenty years following, she sailed the high seas without tragedy. But her journey was drawing to a close – on the Beagle Rocks, Western Australia, she ran aground.

She had been sailing back from Jakarta to Bunbury, but she struck rocks; her propeller gave out and was heavily damaged. Her crew decided that they would take her back to Fremantle for a quick repair job before sending her to Hong Kong, where they would get her fixed fully.

Alas, that was not to be! For as soon as she shuddered her way into the Freemantle docks for repair, in the year 1963, she was mysteriously set fire to. She went ablaze under suspicious circumstances and thousands of dollars were spent, to no avail, to restore her. And therein began her ghost story.

Left abandoned, in the year 1964, there was an attempt to restore The Alkimos. The Pacific Star – another merchant vessel – towed her out to sea, but it was then arrested halfway, since The Pacific Star owed money to a Manila based company. This meant that The Alkimos was left anchored between the Eglington Rocks, around 4 kilometers south of Yanchep Beach, sitting there forlornly on the waters, waiting for a rescue.

As the legal proceedings of The Pacific Star took place, once again, The Alkimos was set fire to. No one knows the story behind both fires – who set the ship ablaze? Why? How? We can only speculate.

Some say that the tragedy that follows the ship can be traced all the way back to its construction; as the ship welders were hurrying to finish the construction for the War, some of them were sealed in between the hulls, unable to get out.

Stuck inside, crawling for space, they probably ran out of air and slowly choked to death. You can imagine the horror of such a death – they slowly ran out of air and then one day, passed out and then passed away.

Obviously, accounts of the tale vary and there is little evidence, but experts say that the ghosts of these trapped souls prevent anyone from salvaging the ship. And if that wasn't enough, here's another tragedy that happened on board.

In 1944, a murder took place on the ship that was apparently hidden from the general public. The story is that the Wireless Operator of the ship – a woman of Canadian origin – was shot dead. Her murderer, a gunnery officer from the crew that was almost entirely Norwegian, then proceeded to shoot himself, making it a murder-suicide.

Remember, this incident took place before The Alkimos was christened as such; she was still Viggo Hansteen at this point, but her tragic luck was already under its way. The incident didn't come to light until a number of tourists reported an apparition, who later came to be known as 'Harry'.

Was this the work of those restless spirits, angry to be trapped and wanting vengeance even then? We can only wonder. For instance, as the crewmembers tried to salvage her for the first time, they reported that the tools they were using began to move around.

A tool would go missing at one part of the ship and then reappear in another. To make matters worse, she passed hands again and again – around 8 times, she was sold and resold, and a number of people tried to restore her.

Every single person who bought her suffered years of terrible luck. Some of her owners went utterly broke and were forced to declare bankruptcy. Others fell seriously ill.

The most disturbing thing here is the fact that as soon as they bought the ship, misfortune would befall them. And the moment they sold it and it left their hands, their bad luck would magically disappear. Anyone who fell sick, recovered. Anyone who lost money regained it.

These chilling tales are accompanied by the stories that the frightened crewmembers swear by – any salvage crew that stayed on the ship to help restore her, refused to go out of their cabins alone. They kept hearing soft footsteps and random, mysterious smells – as though someone was cooking – would appear on the ship, even when there was no chef or even kitchen around.

If the crewmembers went looking for the source of the smell, it would vanish. But the moment the gallery doors closed, the smells would come right back.

There was another crew on the ship – one that was working on its own time. Only, this wasn't a living crew and it didn't breathe like the salvage men did; they didn't work with them, but they certainly kept them terrified. Misfortune followed all those who bought The Alkimos – for instance, a married couple who owned her lost their baby. The pregnant woman slipped on deck and had to be rushed to the hospital, but alas, it was too late; her baby was stillborn.

But it wasn't until the year 1964 that The Alkimos became a shipwreck. Tragedy followed her – this was when she ran aground all by herself. No human being ran her into the rocks and reports suggest that the weather was not strong enough to have pushed her into them.

Still, somehow, she ran amok and the back of the ship broke; she sank into the waters and when she was engulfed, she was officially declared a wreck.

No human or natural intervention, and yet, she sank – is this the work of the mystery, ghost crew? Were they trying to release themselves from their trapped state by somehow pushing her into the waters? One can only wonder.

Since she was submerged, The Alkimos has become a landmark site on the Indian Ocean. Several people have dared to venture into the wreck to find out what truly happened; needless to say, few of these incidents ended well. It turned into a series of injuries, mysterious disappearances and even some deaths.

Here's an interesting tidbit – author Jack Sue, curious and skeptical, decided to explore the wreck and write about it. In the course of his research, he fell seriously ill, but he did manage to publish his book, 'The Ghost of Alkimos', wherein he writes that horses refuse to go anywhere within a 500m distance of the wreck site!

It seems that the animal kingdom can perceive what we humans cannot.

Till the April of 2007, one could see the ship from the beach. But it has, since then, disintegrated and completely vanished. But it's veritably not a case of out of sight, out of mind – the area of the wreck is dangerous and plagued with bad luck.

Ships that pass by, experience mysterious engine failures, tourists that pass by on boats fall overboard and many people get injured when they get close to it. Too many people have even had brushes with death – there are a number of stories of people going overboard and almost drowning close to the wreck site.

And if that's not enough to convince you – locals report that an apparition comes around often, dressed in nothing but oilskin. He walks around the beach area close to The Alkimos wreck site, but any attempts to find or follow him inevitable fails and even leads to disaster.

Initially believing him to be a hermit, some people decided to search for him; they had spotted him just a few minutes before they decided to follow and find him. But it was in vain; he vanished. Assuming that he took refuge on the ship, parts of which were still floating above water at that point, they went to the wreck – there was nothing and no one there.

From Perth, went a long-distance swimmer, well known for his abilities. He was strong enough that he could swim even while towing a bag filled with 'Emu Export Beer Cans'.

But, he went missing close to the wreck (on a course from Cottesloe to Rottnest Island) and years later; it was his skull that was found. And it was found within the wreck of The Alkimos.

So is all this the work of the mystery ghost crew trapped within the hull? Are they taking out their anger in a malevolent manner, lashing out against anyone in their vicinity, tortured and trapped, as they have been for so many decades together? We can only wonder...

CHAPTER 8

ON THE HIGHWAY TO HELL – TUEN MUN ROAD

When you think of a haunted place, you usually imagine a lonely, deserted, dark place that people are terrified to frequent. Tuen Mun Road will prove you wrong. In Hong Kong is a 12-mile expressway that is extremely busy and yet, extremely haunted.

Hong Kong is one of the busiest, business-oriented cities in the whole world. The Tuen Mun is, in fact, one of the most used expressways within the city, infamous for how it has been built. It is located right next to steep terrain and the expressway runs all along the coastline of Hong Kong.

Obviously, a haunting cannot happen without a tragedy. The tragedy here is the steep terrain – given how dangerous it can be to traverse, it's not surprising that a number of horrific accidents have taken place in this area.

What's interesting is that not all people believe that these accidents are completely accidental – some say that the highway has a flaw in design that has led to so many deaths. Others say that it's due to poor maintenance, combined with bad weather, blind spots and narrow lanes.

Whatever the reason, the fact remains – the highway, opened to public transport in the year 1977, remains a veritable spot of accidents and deaths. For the past 3 decades, a number of tragic instances have taken place, leading it to become a bed of paranormal activity.

A number of cars that have been wrecked have had gruesome experiences; drivers who narrowly escaped death claim by supernatural activity and not poor maintenance or even bad weather.

On the 10th of July in the year 2003, a truck on the expressway went out of control suddenly. It crashed into a passenger bus – around 22 people, including the bus driver, were killed instantly and the bus plunged over the 115 feet drop below the road. This made history as one of the most tragic and horrific accidents to have ever happened in Hong Kong. Maps, figures and statistics show that the roads are poorly constructed and are narrow enough that the accident could be explained by science.

But the fact that such accidents keep happening repeatedly is testament to the fact that something is not right and this something cannot be explained by normal science. So what makes Tuen Mun Road so dangerous? Wherein lies its horror?

Locals swear that any of the accidents that happen on this highway are caused by the haunted spirits of the people who have already been killed in gruesome manners on the road. As one speeds across the road, one sees a strange apparition. Needless to say, one brakes sharply and then, often lost control of the vehicle on a road that looks easily wide and comfortable to drive on.

This, many believe, is one reason why the bus accident happened that day – the truck driver saw an apparition emerge randomly in the middle of the road and he lost control of his vehicle, slamming into the bus, thereby killing so many.

And the cycle continues; the more the deaths, the more the trapped ghosts and the worse the hauntings. Locals believe that these spirits, trapped because of a senseless tragedy, are lashing out in anger – they want to take revenge on humanity for having put them there through no fault of their own. Thus, more and more accidents take place on a road that should, ideally, be safe. Drivers are terrified into either slamming into other vehicles or crashing to their own deaths.

Investigations have been conducted regularly to try and identify why there are so many accidents on the Tuen Mun Road. Science shows that there are no real reasons – and anything that survivors quote is written off as imagination. Some drivers say that they saw glowing eyes in the bushes that distracted them, leading them to have serious crashes on the road.

And it's not just the local truck drivers – tourists have also seen these glowing eyes and have been terrified by them. Others swear by the apparitions and state that they couldn't take their eyes off the strange figures, thus leading to so many accidents.

Paranormal activity over the world has shown that the spirits tend to want to increase their own kind. Perhaps they are acting out – they are so angry for being killed so needlessly that they take the life of the first person they see, thus continuing the cycle. They live out their tragic ends again and again, sadistically taking revenge for their untimely deaths.

There is another road as scary as the Tuen Mun Road in Scotland, between Gretna Green and Dumfriesshire. Also named 'The Ghost Road', people have seen a number of apparitions on this path and strange accidents keep happening here, as unexplained and bizarre as the Tuen Mun Road itself.

For instance, in the year 2000, a woman named Donna Maxwell was coming back home from her mother's place; the night was calm and clear and she stated that everything was fine. That is, until a strange man randomly appeared in front of her car from out of nowhere. She slammed the brakes, terrified of hitting him, but before she could do anything, he vanished.

Shaken, she went to the police, worried about having hurt or killed him, but hours of searching led to the police finding absolutely nothing. So shaken was she by this instance, she decided never to take that road again, and even today, uses only the bypass to travel.

This account is so uncannily similar to the Tuen Mun Road that you can't help but identify the patterns in which the paranormal works. The trapped spirits, perhaps looking for release and the sweet embrace of eternal sleep, appear on the roads – are they pleading for help?

Or are they malevolent, wanting vengeance? In either case, all they do is terrify the drivers in causing more senseless tragedy – it's a never-ending cycle that only continues into the infinite.

CHAPTER 9

ON THE RAILS AT THE MEXICO CITY METRO

'El Metro' – the Mexico City Metro as it's called – is infamous for the haunted subways it boasts. A number of people have met their end in these subways, trapping them here for eternity, restless and angry. What is ironic, if you think about it, is that a subway is essentially a passageway that leads you to another destination; to be trapped within it must be horrific.

Of these many subways, the busiest terminal is the Tasquena station in Mexico. Not only is it a subway terminal, it is also the home port of a number of other public transport circuits such as the city buses, the light rail and even publicly run mini vans.

Obviously, hundreds of people come to this terminal to catch their preferred mode of transport and go into their work or home or wherever they are headed to.

Another interesting fact about the terminal is that it is one of the closest terminals to the city bus station. Anyone who wants to travel to the south or is arriving from the south knows that these this exchange of transport is vital – the terminals are not connected to each other, as it would be in the US or in Europe, which means that passengers must make a lengthy walk to make the exchange.

In between the bus and the train stations, you have a number of small shops and vendors – the subway also has a huge hangar where the trains that need repair are sent.

Why am I telling you all this? Because I want to explain to you just how large this place is and how easy it is for one to get hopelessly lost

35

within. And night times are said to be very dangerous, thanks to the high rate of crime.

A number of people have stated that they met an old man on their travels during the nighttime. He asks them if he can walk with them through the subway and give them company; in the dark, one is always happy to have another person around.

Some agreed to have him come along because they wanted to help a poor old man – whatever the reason, they all went with him. The man always walks in shadows so that people get only glimpses of his face and once they reach the subway stairs that leads to the other side, he tells them that he will walk on ahead and they can join him outside. When they emerge, he is long gone, leaving you behind all by yourself.

Many people believe that this old man is the spirit of a man murdered in the subway. If he is indeed, a ghost, it's interesting to note that he is not malevolent – unlike most spirits that haunt a place, he chooses to lead lost passengers back to the light, since he himself has been trapped down there without release for such a long time. He has made it his mission to make sure that no one else remains lost like he is.

It seems that there is hope, even for ghosts and haunted spirits.

Another lost soul is Victor Plantoff, whose story is very interesting too. When inspectors did their routine search during closing time, they kept coming across a man who was not allowed to enter the metro. They questioned him angrily and asked him what he was doing there – he pulled out an ID, claiming to be a Metro Rail worker.

Only – Victor Plantoff, rail worker, had died in the year 1989. He was a subway inspector who had died in the line of duty. It wasn't until this instance that the current officers realized what had happened; Victor was one of the most dutiful officers to have ever worked in the subway. He was never once late to work and he never broke subway protocol while doing his duty – except for once, when he lost his life.

Protocol dictated that the workers walk in the direction opposite to the trains so that they would know when it was coming and not get hurt. The one instance he walked in the same direction as the train, he didn't see it coming – it smashed into him from behind, killing him instantly.

A classic case of unfinished business, Victor never even realized that he was dead; he still comes in to work after 3 a.m. every morning. A number of workers have reported seeing him, but they're never able to pin him down, for he vanishes too quickly.

Like with any subway, this one too has several tragic deaths associated with it. Victims keep jumping front of the oncoming trains to take their own lives – and violent deaths, more often than not, lead to hauntings. These tormented souls, seeking release from life, loose life, but the sleep they crave is still denied to them – they end up trapped on the spot they died and appear as apparitions that terrify the layman.

A number of commuters who take this subway have sworn to being able to communicate with these spirits. Many of them have seen these apparitions, some even on a daily basis; but they turn their head away for a moment and when they turn back, the apparition has vanished, leading them to believe that they were seeing things. People have seen apparitions on the tracks, where the suicide victims jumped to end their lives.

More than the daily commuters, it's the inspectors who collect the corpses of these victims who tell the most disturbing and bizarre stories. Sometimes, when they go down to collect the dead body, a passenger stops them and tells them something kind, like thanking them for the good work they do.

And then, they would go down and have the shock of their lives – the corpse would be of the very person who just stopped and spoke to them...

The Panteones-Tacuba tunnel is yet another terrifying part of the Metro Rail in Mexico. The word Panteones in Spanish can be translated to English as 'graveyards' – yes, that's right, the very name tells you how disturbing it is. The station was named for the two graveyards it lay close to, one of which is a British cemetery and the other Spanish.

As with any graveyard, this one is also accompanied by tales of the paranormal – people swear that they can hear someone knocking on the walls of the tunnels as they pass through. Some have seen shadowy lumps and strange silhouettes in front of them, but when they tried to identify them and get close to them, they vanished into thin air.

Workers who spend all their time in this tunnel speak of how eerie noises, random screams and cries and strange footsteps sound, especially when the time to close work comes upon them. The workers swear that Panteones is one of the most terrifying places to work in; along with the sounds and the restless sense of the spirits, they often feel like they are being followed.

And if that isn't enough to convince you about the paranormal hotspot that the Mexican Metro Rail is, consider this. The stations between Zocalo and Allende is a regular sight of the empty train that passes by without fail every morning at 3 a.m.

The train doesn't stop anywhere, just running down the line before it vanishes at dawn. Locals believe that this is the ghost train from the accident that happened on this line in the year 1975 – more than 30 people were killed. Obviously, such needless tragedy is bound to have left a mark, especially given the mysterious circumstances under which the accident happened.

Of the many stories in the Mexican Metro Rail, these are the five most infamous legends. Whether they are true or not – it's up to you to believe. But one cannot deny that there is something within the dark that roams at nights; they don't seem to be malevolent, but they do embody the sense of the other that we can't really comprehend.

CHAPTER 10

A PRISON RIOT IN NEW MEXICO STATE PENITENTIARY

A prison is always a place of mayhem and havoc and the New Mexico State Penitentiary saw for itself how depraved things could get in the hands of prisoners.

In the year 1980, some high security prisoners managed to escape their jail sentence and then took over the entire prison – for 36 long hours, they used the prison grounds as their own playpen, making it the deadliest prison riot in the history of the USA.

As the 70s drew to a close, the Penitentiary had become extremely crowded. They were always understaffed and what guards they did have had little to no training. The 'Snitch System' in place was not something the inmates were fond of and the protest levels amongst them were on the rise.

Worse still was the manner in which the prison wardens ignored the complaints – bad food, overcrowding, lack of good education services and the like were getting the prisoners angry but the wardens ignored them and went on with things as they were.

Perhaps they should have paid closer attention – the ticking time bomb maybe could have been prevented. But they didn't, and things came to a head soon enough.

On a Friday evening, the inmates were gathered around, drinking the cheap prison alcohol they were given. These particular criminals were supposed to be in high and maximum security areas, but their cells were still under construction, which meant that they had been housed in the normal dorm cells with the rest of the inmates. Drunk and annoyed, a small riot broke out between them as they fought amongst themselves.

The guards on duty at this time were inexperienced. And they were also very few in number – it didn't take long before the criminals overpowered these men. They took away the prison keys and without hesitation, the inmates went straight to the prison pharmacy, aiming for the drugs stored within.

The criminals who had started the riots roped in the other prisoners as well – together, this growing group made its way to Cell Block 4. This was where all the 'snitches' had been placed; each of them had been given an individual cell for their own safety. On a normal day, one couldn't break into these cells. Today, however, one of the workers had left behind a welding torch and the prisoners used that to cut the cell doors open.

For all that they were mad at the snitches, you wouldn't expect them to go beyond beating them up, perhaps. But we forget – these prisoners were meant to be maximum security for a reason; they were the worst kind of criminals, ready to do anything for their own satisfaction. In that case, then, it shouldn't really come as a surprise what they did next – they cut the doors open and then burnt the snitches alive.

To this day, on the walls, you can see the outline of a snitch trying to escape the fire.

What's deeply disturbing about this outline is that it has been rubbed off innumerous times – each time that it is rubbed off, cleaned and then painted over, it comes back, dark and perfectly outlined, as though to remind the prisoners that there were people behind those snitches; real life people who had been ruthlessly murdered for trying to save themselves.

On the night of the riot, almost 33 prisoners were murdered. And not all of them were snitches – there was one man who had been kept in the snitches section for his own safety. He was a prisoner who was mentally ill and since that section was the safest section of the prison, he had been kept there. His was the most gruesome death of all – his head was severed from his body and then placed on a rolling cart as a message for all to see.

A number of criminals died of drug overdoses. And then the prison gym was set ablaze – inmates and guards alike were trapped inside, all dying a suffocating, painful death.

For two days, this madness continued before the criminals could be subdued. Despite all the trauma they caused, however, no prisoner was convicted for the deaths of so many inmates and guards – the survivors were transferred to other jails.

It goes without saying the penitentiary was closed down completely after this incident happened. A new maximum-security jail was opened right across from the old building, which is now called 'The Old Main'. Today, that building is used as a storehouse, where props and other things are kept. It remains closed, however, given how it is one of the most haunted spots within the country.

Given its bloody history, it's not surprising that people would want to use it in films. When shooting was taking place here, however, inexplicable paranormal activity happened; the cameras even caught some of these instances on film.

For a long time, the general public had no access to the building; one paranormal group was allowed to shoot a Halloween special inside the building and though the media that went in were skeptic, they came out completely changed and traumatized.

The Old Main doesn't have any electricity, given that the building has been vacant for ages. When the group entered, they were startled to hear the sound of all the cell doors slam shut. One after another, the doors went bang-bang in the dark; the sound was caught on tape too.

What's even more disturbing is that these doors could only be opened or closed with electricity – if you had to move them manually, they would take a very long time to open or close. Large metal wheels had to be cranked open to move them; these wheels were utterly rusted and useless, and without electricity, there was no way in which the doors could have opened and shut so fast. Remember, the building didn't have electricity.

The reason there is so much controversy surrounding this is that an investigation was conducted and little evidence turned up. The doors were all shut tight, but no one knew how it had happened. One investigator went inside before the building was opened to public tours and she reported that she didn't feel any negative vibes; what's surprising is that she's one of the most experienced and sensitive paranormal investigators there is.

So the skeptic can feel validated – until she came to the prison's gas chambers. This was where she could feel negative vibes the most.

During a film shoot here, the producer decided to play a prank on one of his young actors, who was doing only a small role in his film. The two of them walked around the Old Main together at night with a flashlight and they went straight into Cell Block 4.

They headed for the place where the indents from beheading the mentally ill inmate were still visible. The producer pointed out the black burnt outline of the prisoner and then dared the actor to spend a night at the Gas Chamber. The actor agreed and the producer led him down the flight of stairs to the basement where the chamber is located.

At the end of the corridor, the two men saw a small light – there was a candle that had been lit, placed in the area that was used to oversee executions. The actor believed that it was the producer's prank, but the latter denied any knowledge of the candle. Now scared, the producer insisted they return, but the actor sat down on the viewing chair from which all executions could be seen clearly.

The actor turned to his producer and he saw that the man's eyes were wide-struck and staring at something behind him; he turned to see a number of dark figures staring back at them from the shadows, a sense of malevolence in the air. Without another word, the two of them jumped up and fled down the hall, completely shaken.

After this, a number of videos have been shot here and many investigations have taken place to see if there was any truth to these men's claims.

And there does seem to be – a riot and a massacre such as this one could not go without leaving a mark. The aftermath of all that horror and pain still linger; these dark forms are perhaps the prisoners, waiting for a release that they never got to see in real life.

When they were alive, they were trapped in there for crimes they committed – now, in death; they are trapped forever through no fault of their own.

CHAPTER 11

THE DEATHLY DREAM OF HOLLYWOOD

The United States of America has, over the years, become synonymous with the towering Hollywood Sign on Mount Lee. First built in the year 1923, the Hollywood sign was meant to actually advertise a real estate company that was based out of the Beachwood Canyon.

Each letter of H-O-L-L-Y-W-O-O-D stands at 50 feet of height and a width of 30 feet. Originally made out of wood, the sign read 'Hollywoodland' and it was actually supposed to be a temporary advertisement marker that has, since then, become infamous.

By the time the year 1939 rolled around, the sign was falling to shambles, no longer maintained. The land was given away to the government – the sign passed hands to become property of the Las Vegas city and the Hollywood Chamber of Commerce decided to rebuild it as their own.

Hollywood, by this time, had become famous and they decided that it would embody them. Till the 70s, this new sign reigned, after which it was abandoned, until some concerned citizens took up fundraising for it and ended up rebuilding it with steel.

What is not very well known about the sign is that it's haunted. A young woman's apparition has been seen around it many times – people believe that it is the ghost of Millicent Lillian Entwistle, often known as Peg.

Her story is one of tragedy – born in the year 1908 in Wales, she was raised by her father and her brothers since her mother passed away when she was very young. They moved to New York, where she set

44

her heart on being an actress.

But this woman's life was not meant to be happy – soon after the move, her father was run over by a car and died. Her brothers moved away to California, where they stayed with their uncle; Peg, wanting to pursue her dream, stayed back in New York and struggled as an actor.

At the young age of 17, however, she landed her first acting role – she was placed in a Boston based repertory company, which took her to Broadway. She soon became a famous comedienne and in the year 1927, she got married to Roland Richey, who was almost a decade older than her.

The marriage was a sham – Richey had already been married to another woman, and had six children before Peg. She filed for divorce, but didn't entirely let go of him; she offered him money to pay the alimony to his first wife and kept him out of jail.

It was around this time that one of her productions; 'Mad Hopes' brought her a lot of recognition. But the fame wouldn't last long; soon after, when she moved to LA, she lost her status as a recognized actor and had to get by with odd jobs. The infrequent bookings for her shows worsened her financial condition and she had no choice but to follow her brothers to her uncle's place.

Eventually, though, she caught a break – she was cast in the film the Thirteen Women, with Irene Dunne.

But it was not meant to be either...

Her work in the movie was not at all welcomed; she was fired and her contract was terminated. Without work and her acting skills under heat, Peg fell into subsequent depression and became an alcoholic to boot. She moved back with her uncle and then in the September of 1932, she told him that she was going out to meet a few friends.

She walked up to Mount Lee and removed her coat and her purse. She placed both on the letter 'H' and then climbed up a maintenance ladder. At the very top, she breathed in deeply and then took the plunge straight to her death – she was barely 24 years old.

A hiker came across her purse and her coat and then discovered her body at the bottom. Worried about getting caught up in a case he had no interest in, he took her suicide note, wrote an anonymous note of his own with the details of her corpse's location and left it along with her belongings at the police station.

Ever since, Peg has been haunting the Hollywood Sign. A number of people who hike in the area have seen her – they describe her as a beautiful blonde woman who appears around Griffith Park. She looks extremely sad, sources claim, and whenever someone tries to talk to her, she simply vanishes. People who walk their pets within the area state that their animals act strangely when she's around.

Sometimes, they aren't able to see her at all, only smell her perfume. When they do see her, they see different forms of her – some see the sad, forlorn soul while others see the slightly drunk, depressed and manic version that plunged to her death.

Park Ranger John Arbogast is the biggest evidence of Peg; he has seen her many times. He states that she always smells of gardenias; he tells stories of how the motion sensor alarms to prevent people from killing themselves often go off on their own, even when there is no one in the vicinity.

When John goes to check the sensor, there is no one there, even though they clearly display someone apparently standing less than 5 feet away, ready to take the literal plunge.

Peg's dreams and ambitions went unfulfilled, like so many other starving artists who struggle. Her death is one of senseless tragedy and a loss of passion; but even after she died, she still hangs around the thing she loves the most. Hollywood was her dream – perhaps she is now reaching for it in the aftermath of a shattered dream that even now keeps her trapped and lost.

CHAPTER 12

ROOMMATES OF THE PARANORMAL KIND AT THE NORMANDIE APARTMENT

Imagine – you are all alone in your cozy little apartment, when suddenly, you hear loud yells, panicked screams and shrill cries. You jump in fear, look around franticly for the source of the tortured crowd, only to find nothing there – neither inside your apartment, nor out in the street.

Or… Maybe you just couldn't see the people screaming.

The Normandie Apartment is a place on earth that is utterly haunted; a number of students and professionals have taken it up at cheap rates, happy to get a good bargain. But all good things come at a price; this one was, perhaps, too steep to pay!

Windows would burst open at random instances and then slam shut – it left the tenants shaking in fear, unable to even go to sleep at night.

Like all haunted spots, the house also has a terrifying past, one that replays itself practically every single night. Is the house trying to communicate the horror it has seen over the years? Do the spirits want to escape, want to share how they've been tortured over the decades that they've been trapped inside, unable to get the rest they desire so desperately?

What exactly happened here?

The story begins with the apartment's construction. Built to provide foreign housing, the apartment was purchased in the year 1942 by the daughter of a banker who went by the name of HH Kung. The daughter, whose name was Kung Ling Wei, moved into the house and soon, it became famous for celebrities in China, like Wang Wenjuan,

Wu Yin, Wang Renmei, Qin Yi, Sun Daolin, Zheng Juni, etc., stayed in it one after another.

But soon after the rich people abandoned this apartment, strange things began.

Until the year 1963, the house was left abandoned – finally, actress Shangguan Yunzhu, who was once a star in the 1940s, took over the seventh floor and lived there. Now, her history is rather interesting. Yunzhu, who had been very popular in the 40s, lost her sheen as the 60s crept around, to the point where she even had rebel factions against her in China.

Labeled a reactionary and having her films denounced was nothing short of excruciating for the actor, who was terrified that she would lose everything, jumped out the window of the seventh floor and took her own life, at least ensuring that she would never be forgotten. On the 22nd of November 1968, the actor's death made the news and from there began the trouble.

The next couple of years, the apartment remained empty. But was it truly devoid of all occupants? We don't think so – her neighbors claimed that they could always feel the late actress's presence within the apartment. At nights, especially during the autumn season, they would be able to smell the sudden scent of her perfume – Neroli and ylang ylang –, which would waft across.

With such disturbing reports coming in, research was undertaken to see why these things were happening. Older residents of the apartment, even before the actor killed herself, swore being victims of bizarre instances – one old journalist, Zhou, stated that he could hear multiple footsteps padding around the house through the day, but there was no source.

Others said that they could hear voices; if it was only the actor who took her own life here, then what was the source of the other paranormal activity?

And out came the truth – the Normandie apartment wasn't just the hotspot of the actor's tragedy, but others too... The house is known today as 'The Diving Board' – and for good reason. It was a prime site during China's Cultural Revolution.

For those who don't know, there was a movement in China between 1966-76, started by the then Chairman of the Communist Party, Mao Zedong, who wanted to promote communist beliefs over the capitalism that he thought was overtaking Chinese thought. He sought to bring the art and culture of China down to its grassroots level and make the economy one of power and strategy.

He brought together several Red Guard groups in China, who went around charging people for being enemies of the state. Anything that they believed promoted what they claimed were the traditional Chinese thought, they targeted – all the intellectuals, the artists, actors, anyone with any connection to cultural thought, they were all persecuted and some even harassed to death.

The Normandie house became 'The Diving Board' because these new revolutionaries had driven a number of these State Enemies into the building, from where they jumped off to escape being further harassed and hurt. The Red Guard renamed the house 'The Revisionist Tower'.

The truth is that no matter what name it goes by, the place is a spot of tragedy and horror – people were literally pushed over the edge and fell to their deaths for simply believing in something that was different than what the State wanted them to believe.

It's no wonder that the story still lives on here. Most people around the area report time and again how there is the sound of something heavy crashing onto the street below. It doesn't take a stretch of the imagination to understand what it is – the sound of someone falling to their death and then hitting the pavement once and for all.

People also hear the sound of a woman screaming and wailing, which then morphs into more than one voice begging and then crying for help.

When the residents go to identify the source of the sound, they find nothing. Wood creaks and then breaks late in the night, but in the morning, everything looks just fine; people walking around the house, walking into the windows, crashing against the street – these are all strange sounds that have no source within the apartment itself.

Or perhaps we can say that there seems to be no physical source. For surely, a place that has seen tragedy such as this is bound to be angry and hostile. The presence of the paranormal here is unquestionable – vivid and strange smells, violent and angry screams – they're all very common.

Are these the restless spirits trying to reach out in the wake of their gruesome deaths? Are they trying to tell us their stories or take revenge on the residents for being persecuted through no fault of their own?

One can but imagine what the truth is...

CONCLUSION

The world that we live in, as I have said previously, is a mysterious one. We don't truly comprehend every part of it – the human understanding of it is miniscule at best! Too many things exist that we cannot quantify with our limited perception.

Each place that we saw in this book has a story to tell; just like them, there are hundreds of other places out there, some discovered, some not. But all share a history and all share one common trait – they are part of something bigger, something that is beyond all of us. Some are saddled with pain and sadness, some with anger, and yet others even seem to be happy – in the end, we may never truly understand what goes on behind the scenes.

More often than not, laymen like us don't perceive this other – we are not sensitive enough to understand these spirits and we can only catch angry glimpses of those souls eternally trapped and looking for release. We can't possibly comprehend the magnitude of their suffering; it's best we leave them alone and not tempt our fate.

To shrug off these stories as simply urban legend would be a fool's choice – whether you accept it or not, strange things that aren't completely explained by science do exist and they seem to actually happen all around us!

To quote Deepak Chopra, *"The strange thing about the paranormal is that no matter how often you prove it, it always remains unproven."*

Call it legend, call it myth – there is something out there we cannot understand. In the biggest of tropes – we are not alone.

Thank you so much for downloading this book. I hope you found it intriguing and chilling to read about truly haunted places from across the globe!

If you enjoyed this book, do you think you could leave me a review on Amazon? Just search for this title and my name on Amazon to find it. Thank you so much, it is very much appreciated!

OTHER BOOKS WRITTEN BY ME

Below you'll find some of my other popular books that are popular on Amazon and Kindle as well. You can visit my author page on Amazon to see other work done by me. (Max Mason Hunter).

Unexplained Phenomena

Unexplained Phenomena – Book 2

Bizarre True Stories

True Paranormal

True Paranormal – Book 2

True Paranormal – Book 3

True Ghost Stories And Hauntings

True Ghost Stories And Hauntings – Book 2

True Ghost Stories And Hauntings – Book 3

True Paranormal Hauntings

True Paranormal Hauntings – Book 2

True Paranormal Hauntings – Book 3

True Paranormal Hauntings – Book 4

You can simply search for these titles on the Amazon website with my name to find them.

LIBRARY BUGS BOOKS

Like books?

Would you like them delivered to you every week?

Do you like non-fiction books on a huge range of different topics?

We send out e-books every week so we can share our books with the world!

We have books every week on AMAZON that we send to our email list. If you want in, then visit the link below to sign up and sit back and wait for new books to be sent straight to your inbox!

It couldn't be simpler!

www.LibraryBugs.com

If you want books delivered straight to your inbox, then visit the link above and soon you'll be receiving a great list of e-books every week!

Enjoy :)